AMY GARNER

All The Words Ran Free

Copyright © 2023 by Amy Garner

All rights reserved. No part of this publication may be reproduced, stored or transmitted in any form or by any means, electronic, mechanical, photocopying, recording, scanning, or otherwise without written permission from the publisher. It is illegal to copy this book, post it to a website, or distribute it by any other means without permission.

Amy Garner asserts the moral right to be identified as the author of this work.

First edition

This book was professionally typeset on Reedsy.
Find out more at reedsy.com

Contents

Acknowledgement	1
Preface	2
Beginnings	3
Shawshank	4
The Gram	5
Treats	6
A Working Day	7
Too Much	8
Head Sprain	9
Storming	10
Refund	11
The Fear	12
The Pink River Dolphin	13
Inspirational	15
Swan Song	16
Oxymoron	17
My Anxious Thoughts as an Energetic Meerkat	18
Breakthrough	19
Insomnia	20
A Spaceman Came Travelling	22
Yosemite Cemetery	24
An Edgar Allan Poem	25
People Pleasing	26
Staying In	28
Overthinking	30
Expression	31

Pressure	32
New Year	33
January	34
February 14th	36
March On	37
April's Full	38
Mayhem	39
June	40
D'you Lie?	42
Augustus	43
An Autumn Love Story	45
A Morning Run in Winter	46
Winter Chill	48
Endings	49
Light and Shade	51

Acknowledgement

I dedicate this book to my fellow sensitive souls. May your reflections run deep and your environments be calm.

Thank you to my family and friends for supporting my writing and for being subjected to listening to it on occasion, I really do appreciate you!

Thank you to my dear friend Shona Fordyce, who read the first draft of this book and who regularly inspires me with her sage advice, heart of gold and sharp wit.

To my husband Ross, thank you for your unwavering love and support.

XxX

"Strong Back, Soft Front, Wild Heart"
Dr Brené Brown

Preface

I wish there was a beautifully poetic way of explaining how I write, but I simply find it relaxing to tap out some rhymes on my phone based on whatever is on my mind at the time.

In a world of non-stop notifications and to-do lists, writing allows me to pause and think. In short bursts, often on weekends, I love getting lost in the creative flow of working with words and it feels like, briefly, time stands still.

To share my writing with others is a privilege despite any self doubt that seeps through. Seeing my poems become a tangible book makes it all the more special.

Beginnings

Let's start from the beginning,
A very good place to start.
Putting some thoughts down on paper,
Then ripping them up and apart.

It's alright to know that you're nervous,
It means that you really do care,
Making yourself get out there,
Can begin as a sweaty nightmare.

Starting is always the hard bit,
Not knowing which way to turn.
The middle bit also gets fickle,
And you can't wait to watch it all burn.

But then at the end you'll be ready,
To look back and say that was fun.
And that's when you realise that really,
Your beginnings are never quite done.

Shawshank

I put a poem in my bag,
To keep me company.
But didn't know there was a hole,
   So
   all
   the
   words
   ran free.

The Gram

Those tiny tiles on my black device
Made it seem as though you're chill as ice

Your gorgeous home full of velvet luxe
Made it seem as though you had endless bucks

You were whisked away to exotic lands
And it seemed as though wishes were commands

Your flawless skin and your perfect smile
You were killing it by a country mile

"How do you do it?" I asked one night,
"Create this life and shine so bright?"

"I try so hard," you were softly crying
"But in the end, we're all just trying."

Treats

Add to basket, so much fun!
Go to checkout, nearly done.
Pay with Klarna? Well, why not?
Can just return it, worth a shot.

Confirmation order sent.
Love this recurring event.
Tomorrow I will ooze with zest
And look like her off Pinterest.

Doorbell rings, must be for me!
Cardboard boxes, half a tree.
"Another package?", judge the fam.
Don't blame me, it's Instagram.

Try it on, fold it away
With the rest of my array.
Buzz wore off, "U OK hun?"
Add to basket, so much fun.

A Working Day

Another screen of tiny squares,
Looking out at many stares.
I can't stop glancing at myself,
I think I'm looking like an elf?

"You're on mute mate", always the same,
That phrase, it drives me so insane.
"Can you see me share my screen?"
My keyboard really needs a clean.

"Sorry, need to leave at two,
But I'll send an email through."
I drop a message in the chat,
And leave the meeting, just like that.

So many gripes about the tech,
The Teams fatigue and dodgy neck.
Do you think I have a double chin?
It's all the Zooming out and in.

Too Much

In a bid to be vivacious,
He felt the need to be loquacious.
He tried to be so erudite,
And hated all that could be trite.
His texts could be a disquisition,
He had a quirky disposition.
He tried too hard in his milieu,
And so his friends bid him: "Adieu".

Head Sprain

Cold sweat pours all over me,
Pressure builds just trying to see.
I think my mind is being squeezed,
My left eye has now been seized.
Let me lie down in the dark,
Flashing lights are trying to spark.
Who put my head into a vice?
And cranked it round not once, but twice.
Hours pass and I'm alone,
Slowly the pain starts to groan.
It's waxed and waned just like the moon,
Please let it all be over soon.
Mission done - hijack my brain,
Until next time
Old pal,
Migraine.

Storming

There's a storm in my teacup,
I've left it there to brew.
Now it has become too steeped,
I'm unsure what to do.

I've taken out the teabag,
Added a splash of cold.
Maybe I'll just pour it out,
I'm really far too old.

Refund

"Hello, I'd like a refund please,
No receipt, but I do have these?
Two whole years which do not fit,
The seams have somehow ripped and split.

"I tried to alter here and there,
But now they're in need of repair.
Can I please have an exchange?
I'd like to see another range.

"No returns? But I've been robbed!"
My voice embarrassingly sobbed.
The checkout guy said with concern,
"No need to give yourself heartburn."

"These two years you've learned the most,
Your friend Control was just a ghost.
We don't refund," he flashed a smile,
"So own it all and switch your style."

The Fear

We said goodbye on Friday night,
I walked home, the moon was bright.
As I left, I began to think,
And then my heart started to sink.

The Fear crept up and took her chance,
She grabbed me to begin the dance.
"You said too much," she sneered at me,
"And not enough", she laughed with glee.

I spiralled, then had to agree,
"You're right, I am bad company."
"Remember that joke you tried to make?
What a fail, you massive fake."

I reached my house, pyjamas on,
And thought this can't just be a con?
I had a great time with my friend?
It's *you* driving me round the bend.

The Fear whispered: "But she hates you",
Then my phone buzzed right on cue.
"Hope you made it home ok!!
Next time it's my turn to pay Xx "

The Pink River Dolphin

I am a pink river dolphin.
There aren't very many of me.
I generally keep pretty private,
And don't venture out much to sea.

As I got older I switched out,
My grey to a bright pinky hue.
I found that it worked better for me,
As experiences I did accrue.

I see the grey dolphins all playing,
And putting on a fancy show,
As people take pictures around them,
It's quite the exciting tableaux.

I'd rather stay in my fresh river,
And keep to an intimate group,
Swim away after an hour,
To have time alone to recoup.

I permanently look very happy,
It's the way my mouth's fixed on my face,
But I'm not a show pony of water,
I don't have much social headspace.

My distant friends click: "Come and join us!"
But saltwater isn't for me,
And I feel like a killjoy pink dolphin,
As the rest of them backflip with glee.

I met a young girl one day fishing,
I bobbed up to say my "hello".
She held my pink nose in her small hand,
And this time my smile wasn't faux.

I realised that maybe I'm okay,
My pink is what makes me unique,
And my nature in my quiet river,
Is what adds to my special mystique.

Inspirational

I walked into your hallway,
It had a stenciled dove.
Advice was floating from its beak,
To always LIVE, LAUGH, LOVE

We went into your kitchen,
You'd made us both some toffee.
A sign was hanging on the wall,
To remind you, BUT FIRST, COFFEE

I had to use your toilet,
That very afternoon.
A frame told me to SHOOT FOR STARS,
If I can't land the moon.

With so much inspiration,
There is no place for botching.
I guess that all I can do next,
Is DANCE LIKE NO ONE'S WATCHING

Swan Song

That Swan of yours is too audacious.
He's being really quite flirtatious.
"Calm down mate, and be more gracious,
Plenty room out here, it's spacious."
How can he be so bodacious?
Not OK being this predacious.
He thinks he's being all capacious,
Winning life being tenacious.
His demeanour is fallacious.
"How can you be so rude, salacious?
Back you go, you beast, rapacious,

To your swampy pond, herbaceous."

Oxymoron

Climb down, you maniac,
So we can be alone together.

We'll have an awfully good time,
drinking bittersweet coffee.

We'll eat jumbo shrimp
and go on working holidays.

We'll drink 100% Pure Orange Juice
From Concentrate.

You seem a safe bet,
And I like to gamble responsibly.

My Anxious Thoughts as an Energetic Meerkat

Scurry round and don't stop moving,
Constantly be self-improving,
Always ready, high alert,
Ready to retreat, divert.

I'll be social to a point,
Until I burrow out this joint,
Spine is upright, poker straight,
Tunnel vision, eyes fixate.

Sensing danger every hour,
Standing guard with all my power,
Just stay busy, keep on digging,
Hyper focus, unremitting.

Keep the pace with other critters,
Ignore it when you get the jitters,
This meerkat will not be slowing,
Not when there's this much unknowing.

Breakthrough

I seem to be trapped in my comfort zone,
It's making me feel quite unwell.
Everything's too soft and fluffy,
It's very warm here in my shell.

I seem to be trapped in my comfort zone,
I'm trying to hit quick release.
I'm finding it eerily quiet,
There's something weird with all this peace.

I seem to be trapped in my comfort zone,
I'll break out and face my own fear!
I'll fight and I'll hustle, and flex all my muscles,
And make my own thoughts disappear.

I seem to be trapped in my comfort zone,
But I don't always have to escape.
It's good to step out now and then mate,
But sometimes – you just need a break.

Insomnia

The clock struck nine on Tuesday night.
Time to stop the scroll and avoid blue light.
Just one more minute, said the voice inside.
So I scrolled some more, feeling bleary-eyed.

The clock struck ten on Tuesday night.
Time to wind down now, and do things right.
I brushed my teeth, sprayed lavender mist
And I read my book, smugly ticked my list.

The clock struck eleven on Tuesday night.
Time to nod off and hope with all my might
That my brain turns off, and I drift away.
My thoughts say: 'Nice try, let us run through your day...'

The clock struck twelve on Tuesday night.
My mind is leaping, reaching whole new heights.
Remember that thing you did, and said?
Bet you feel dumb now, lying in this bed.

The clock struck one on Tuesday night.
In four hours' time, the day will get bright.
My thoughts move on to my future days.
And I think: 'Tomorrow I *will* change my ways.'

INSOMNIA

The clock struck two on Tuesday night.
How can this be? This is utter sh*te.
'Just go to sleep!' I whisper scream.
So I think some more about what to dream.

The clock struck four on Tuesday night
And I slowly drift, giving up the fight.
I'm floating now, blissfully asleep,
Then I'm jolted up by a heinous beep.

As the clock struck six on a brand new day
Bags below my eyes are a cloudy grey.
'There's no time for tired!' my thoughts say to me.
'Let's do this then, pass me my CBD.'

A Spaceman Came Travelling

A spaceman came travelling
In 2022,
I met him in the middle
Of a long Aldi queue.
I had no time to speak to him,
He seemed like a real blast,
The checkout guy was throwing,
My weekly shop at me too fast.

That evening I attended
My classes at the gym.
I bumped into the spaceman
Who rocked up on a whim.
He tried to say 'hello' to me,
By the water station,
But my Apple Watch was buzzing
To get back to activation.

The next day I walked to work
With my AirPods in,
The spaceman jumped in front of me,
I punched him in the chin.
I broke my hand and he exclaimed
'Why did you do that dear?',

I didn't know my default blow,
Would bounce off his headgear.

He asked me to sit down a while,
With my hand in bits.
I asked him what he's doing here,
And he said: 'It's the pits,
I fell to Earth and thought I'd try
This modern, newfound place,
But this is all too much for me,
I'm going back to space.'

Yosemite Cemetery

O' Capitan, El Capitan, our stunning trip is done,
Our car survived in all six lanes, the prize – to live – is won.
Hill tops were clear, the bears were near,
The hikers were exulting.
Until they came a tad too close,
And we escaped a pulping.

An Edgar Allan Poem

Once upon a weekend morning, with pyjamas, I adorning,
Over a many Google searches I read such well known lore -
An encyclopaedia - known to us as Wikipedia -
I entered a deep dive of Poe's work I'd never read before.
Quoth the Raven "Nevermore".

My connection did grow stronger, hesitating then no longer,
So I found a *Simpsons* YouTube clip of Homer being Poe.
In my bed with coffee sipping, further I felt myself slipping,
In to a 'Dream within a Dream' which I had never read before.
"Of a surf-tormented shore".

Open here I flung the curtain, when with knowing I was certain,
I had yet much more to know about this gothic guy called Poe.
I continued with my searching, on the sofa now with perching,
I found a 'Tell-Tale Heart' which I had never seen nor read before.
"Villains!" I shrieked, "Dissemble no more!"

Quoth the raven "Nevermore".

People Pleasing

I'd love it if you loved me,
What can I do for you?
I'll be there when you need me,
Anything you ask, I'll do.

Sometimes lines get blurred,
If I try to figure out,
The difference in our preference,
A niggle of self doubt.

It's easy to disguise it,
A cloak of selflessness.
Until my deep resentment,
Is stirred with restlessness.

If I place all my value,
In what you think of me,
Then you have all the power,
And I hand you my key.

It would be so much better,
If we could meet half way,
To lean hard on each other,
So nothing can decay.

PEOPLE PLEASING

It's not an issue you have,
It's mine, and mine alone,
Seek everyone's approval,
And put my worth on loan.

So how can I get past it?
To value you – and me?
To not be so self critical,
And see what others see?

I do not have an answer,
But maybe in good time,
I'll find a way to like us both.
And we will be just fine.

Staying In

It's not that I don't want to,
It's not that I don't care,
It's both a blessing and a curse,
A cross I have to bare.

It's not that I am lonely,
When I need to be alone,
I need to gather up this time,
Or I'll drain down to my bones.

I love those who surround me,
And need to keep you close,
But then I need to step away,
When I've hit the maximum dose.

It really is that simple,
My battery - small, yours - large,
And after some time spent together,
I need plugged in to charge.

So don't worry if I am leaving,
I need time to process,
Our cups are two different sizes,
You want more, while I need less.

STAYING IN

We might come over as quiet,
But we'll listen with such great intent,
And cling on to the words you have spoken,
Time with you - is time well spent.

So if you are also an introvert,
Remember that you're not alone,
Until such a time that you want to,
Retreat, head off, and go home.

Overthinking

A day ago you told me that you were doing fine,
I asked you how your work was, you asked me how was mine.
Then you sent a message, you had to go away,
Would not be back tomorrow, because you weren't okay.

I tried to process slowly and figure it all out,
What did I say or do to you to cause so much self-doubt?
Was it when I asked you for all of that advice?
Next time I'll be quiet, or keep it more concise.

Three days passed and nothing, I didn't hear a word,
So I assumed you were with them, the people you preferred.
Was it when I'd asked you if you would feed my cat?
Your face had said of course you would, like a true diplomat...

It really drove me crazy, not knowing what was wrong.
I made up all these stories and dragged you right along,
Is it narcissism or do I care too much?
It wouldn't be the first time you've called me a soft-touch.

Five days passed and nothing, but then you got in touch.
I asked: 'What has happened?!', and you replied: 'Not much.'
I said that I was sorry for the things I'd said to you.
You did not know what I meant, you'd been in bed with flu.

Expression

I have a small affliction,
That always gives away,
My feelings on a subject,
Words I don't want to say.

There's no way to control it,
When my features displace,
And all my thoughts are written,
So clearly on my face.

Pressure

When are you two getting married?
Must be about that time!
When I tell you what I think,
While you are in your prime.

Oh, you two got married!
That's great, so now crack on,
And have a little baby,
You shouldn't wait too long.

Oh, you had a baby!
What a little dream.
Excited for a sibling?
They'll make a cute wee team.

Each person has their own things,
They need to figure out.
So leave them to their own lives,
Stop filling them with doubt.

My crystal ball is broken,
I've no answers to your query,
Let's talk about something else,
This pressure makes me weary.

New Year

HELLO NEW YEAR AND NEW ME!!
What have you got in store to see?
Is this the year I go plant-based?
Fibre up, with bowels braced.

Is this when I will not hit snooze?
And leap in to my running shoes.
Smash 10k out by sunrise,
And seize each day, those runner's highs.

Is this the year I journal daily?
Learn to play the ukulele?
Will I do a new degree?
Or grow my own organic tea?

Is this when I will learn to sew?
Appreciate a fine Merlot?
Perhaps I'll host a writing group,
And learn to make French onion soup.

It seems unlikely to be fair,
I don't have much more time to spare,
With all these extra plans to cram,
I think I'm OK as I am.

January

Every year it gets us,
A little by surprise,
When January stays for a month,
A Yeti with four eyes.

He starts so optimistic,
With lights still twinkling bright,
The Yeti puts his screens away,
By seven every night.

He makes it seem so easy,
To pack a daily lunch,
Instead of panic buying snacks,
And calling it a brunch.

The Yeti soon gets jaded,
With night starting at three,
His motivation levels match,
His lack of Vitty-D.

He dreams of warmer climates,
Blue sky and trendy sandals,
But now is time to hunker down,
With blankets and some candles.

JANUARY

With every year the Yeti proves,
How lumbering and grey,
The days up to the 31st,
Can be from Hogmanay.

The Yeti is not discontent,
Nor is he unimpressed,
He knows that all he needs this month,
Is work, and play, and rest.

February 14th

I tried to write you a Valentine's rhyme,
To tell you: 'I think that you're simply sublime.'
My words ran together,
Caved under the pressure,
But this limerick arrived just in time.

March On

Is that some blue sky forming?
I'm ready for some light.
I am a coiled spring waiting,
To spring forth overnight.

My Winter wasn't easy,
Stripped down to my last leaf,
Hindsight shows this was a phase,
But Winter is not brief.

Outside the clouds are parting,
My shoots starting to sprout,
I haven't got the energy,
For any more self doubt.

Your seasons will turn also,
And life will throw some hail,
So cling to those there for the storm,
Who hold you as you flail.

Recognise you're strong enough,
To make it through to dawn,
Somehow, some good will come of this,
So look up and March on.

April's Full

I hope that your April is filled to the brim,
With both peaceful moments, and trips on a whim.
With hot buttered toast on those cold rainy days,
And your train getting in without any delays.

With first sips of coffee that soothe to the soul,
With your favourite snacks in your favourite bowl.
Walks with the sun shining down on your face,
And stacks of your books waiting on your bookcase.

With belly-ache laughter and witty retorts,
When hilarity hits and you can't stop the snorts.
With slow weekend mornings, and hard working weeks,
And everyone listening more than they speak.

With days when your thoughts are upbeat and not stressed,
With times when you know that you're doing your best.
With great acts of kindness and nothing uncool,
There just isn't time, because April is full.

Mayhem

Mary had a little lamb,
And on the first of May,
They decided to jet off -
A trip to San Jose.

She smuggled it on to the plane,
It had a snow white fleece.
She got away with making clear,
He was her stress release.

The poor lamb's ears began to pop,
At such high-altitude.
And so began a long-haul flight,
With ovine attitude.

The lamb went mad and gambolled off,
Skipped up and down the aisles,
But Mary couldn't pin him down,
For fifteen thousand miles.

Hours on and they arrived,
In sunny San Jose.
Mary and her little lamb,
Their tickets now one-way.

June

It's a hard road darling,
And there ain't no one,
I'd rather sit right next to.

So take my hand,
hold it strong and tight,
on this Sunday night in June.

When you get too tired,
I'll take on the wheel,
And we'll swap over without fuss,

Love is taking turns,
Driving through the night for us.

We're on this rough terrain,
So full of ups and downs,
Which we are passing through.

So take my hand
Hold it good and tight,
Look on up at the strawberry moon.

When you get too tired,

JUNE

I'll take on the wheel,
And we'll swap over without fuss,

Love is taking turns,
Driving through the night for us.

D'you Lie?

Do you lie to me, when you lie with me?
In our home tucked away, living beside the sea.
Do you see me cry, when I'm trying to try?
We were having such a beautiful time,
So why d'you lie?

Augustus

I have an old man, a crusty old gammon,
Who lives in my head - Augustus McCannon.
He's sharp and he's harsh, and he's never OK,
And he shouts and he judges all night and all day.

I try not to let him get loud and unbearing,
But it's hard with a lodger who's just so uncaring.
He clutters and throws his opinions like glitter,
How can this old man be so sour and bitter?

But why did I let him walk through my front door?
To take up my space, and spread dirt on my floor?
Who let him stay all these years as my critic?
The things that he says, they are simply horrific.

It's time to get out old Augustus McCannon,
You've taken enough, you're a feelings assassin.
You fill me with doubt with my every move,
You will never stop and you'll never approve.

You are not me, and I am not you,
You're a critic by trade, and we're finally through,
I can't seem to chuck you to get this resolved,
So I'll just need to starve you, 'till you have dissolved.

I'll make you much smaller than you want to be,
And make you realise that you're wrong, what you see.
Your outlook is warped, and you're wrong old Augustus,
One day you'll be served with a warm bowl of justice.

An Autumn Love Story

The leaves are turning brown and crispy.
Going out coat-free is risky.
Should I flash an ankle bare?
Short sleeves only if I dare.

I miss you waiting home for me.
'I'll be back soon', I guarantee.
We will watch Netflix together,
When I get in from the weather.

I go outside, the rain does hammer.
My Fall style has lost its glamour.
Minutes in, I'm one drowned rat.
Bad times for my poor suede hat.

I want you, need you, warm me up.
Build me up, my buttercup,
I sprint home at pace - full throttle,
To you my love -

Hot water bottle.

A Morning Run in Winter

I take a step outside my door,
The cold I just cannot ignore.
It bites my lips, I exhale out,
I rid myself of any doubt.

My vision blurred, I start to jog,
I navigate through all this fog.
Through the park, I nod hello,
To fellow runners on the go.

The cold air pierces through my lung,
I pass the schoolkids, backpacks slung.
The beat, it pulses through my ears,
As daylight slowly reappears.

Halfway round, over the bridge,
I dream of what's inside my fridge.
With each breath leaves a foggy trail,
This temperature is off the scale.

5k – and I've made it home,
End my early morning roam.
Heart rate slows, and breathing calms,
I rub my white and frozen palms.

A MORNING RUN IN WINTER

Now the best bit of the day,
Knowing it is out the way.
Sipping coffee from my mug,
Feeling, oh, so very smug.

Winter Chill

I tossed a poem on the fire,
To stave the frosty chill.
The words burned slow, an orange glow,
To save my heating bill.

Endings

Happily ever after, the ending began,
The perfect conclusion for a keen Disney fan,
But what happened next to those fairytale dreams?
When reality hit and it tugged at the seams.

Sleeping Beauty, Prince Philip - they went castle hunting,
But the tough bidding market was just so confronting.
They managed to settle a three-bedroom flat,
With no double glazing and a white Persian cat.

Cinderella, Prince Charming, they started off well.
They certainly seemed under each other's spell.
But time wore them down and they had to admit,
His shoe fetish meant - it just wasn't a fit.

Aladdin and Jasmine flew off on their carpet,
But Al missed the hum and the buzz of the market.
They tried long distance, but both started to suffer,
So not before long, they ghosted each other.

On to Ariel and Eric, our pair from the sea,
They have a daughter, a wee girl - Melody.
They call their small team the 'three musketeers',
But Ariel and Eric haven't slept in four years.

And lastly, to finish - we have Belle and the Beast,
They moved to a bungalow, in the North East.
They've found a good group, a rowdy young rabble,
And they spend Sunday nights playing fierce games of scrabble.

With fairy-tale endings, they're fully 2-D,
It puts lots of pressure on us, you and me.
To learn in our youth, things will always be great,
Just doesn't allow for when life says 'checkmate'.

Light and Shade

The Sun lost patience with the Moon,
'When is my time to shine?'
The waxing crescent said: 'Just wait,
And soon you'll get your time.'

The Sun got mad and burned with rage,
'I want to shine my light.'
The Moon stayed calm and said: 'Not yet,
Right now I'm glowing bright.'

In time the Sun began to rise,
It confidently beamed.
The Moon slept softly at the back,
And quietly it dreamed.

The hours passed and soon it was,
Time for the Sun to set.
It made a scene, turned up the heat,
And caused the sky to sweat.

'My friend,' the Moon gently explained,
'There is a time for you,
To show the world your brightest rays,
And give the world your view.'

'Time will move on and shadows start,
To cast darkness abound,
So there's no point in stropping,
When it's my turn to come around.'

'With every light, there must be dark,
So let your brightness fade,
Of course go forth and shine away,
But let there be some shade.'

Printed in Great Britain
by Amazon